NATIONAL GEOGRAPHIC

T0308165

Body Beasts

PATHFINDER EDITION

By Peter Winkler

CONTENTS

2 Body Beasts

8 Seeing Tiny Creatures

10 A Closer Look

12 Concept Check

Body

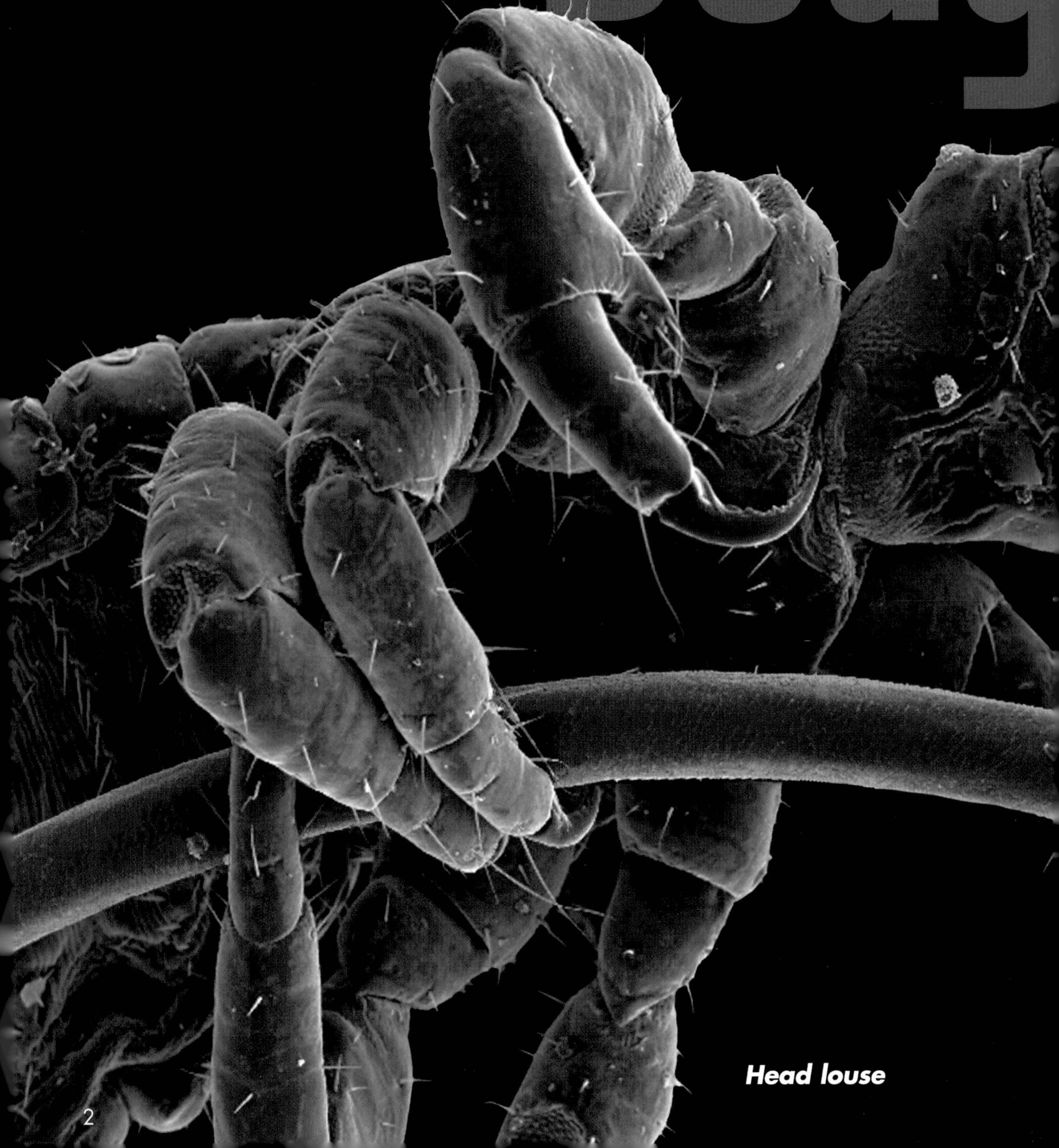

Head louse

Beasts

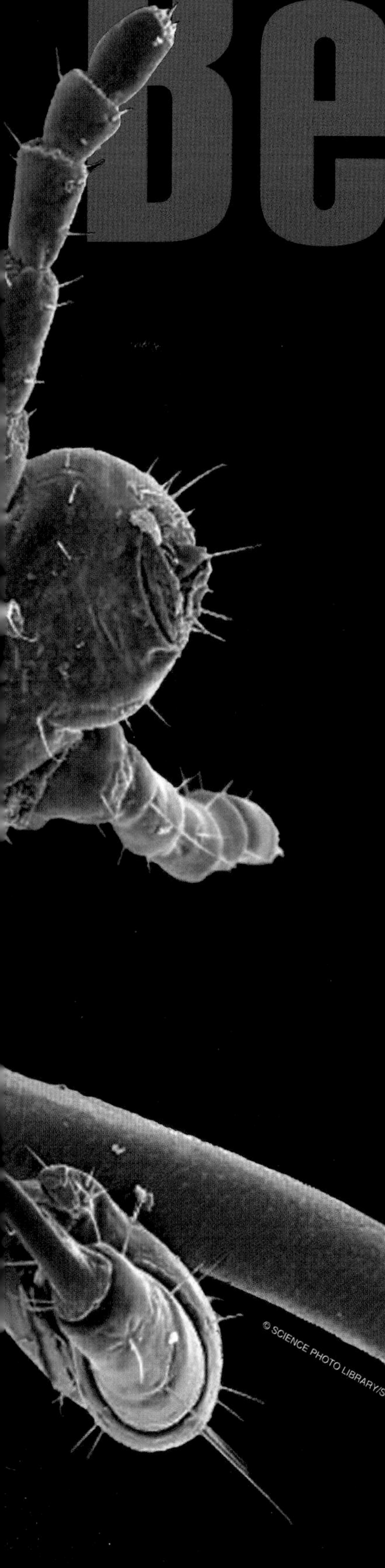

© SCIENCE PHOTO LIBRARY/SCIENCE SOURCE

Animals live in habitats. You know that. But did you know that animals can also be habitats for other living things?

By Peter Winkler

Human beings and other animals are never alone. We always have plenty of company. Lots of tiny living things call our bodies home. To them, a body is a world of habitats. A habitat is a place where things can live.

Some of these wee neighbors are harmful. Most, though, don't really affect **hosts.** Some actually help. Indeed, many animals would have trouble living without them!

So who are these tiny body beasts? Let's see.

Lousy Guests

Lice may be the best known body beasts. These small insects live in a host's hair. The louse's six legs grab a hair and hold on tight.

Lice generally stay close to the scalp. Their spear-like teeth jab the skin. Blood then squirts into the insect's mouth.

Louse bites usually do not hurt. But the insect's **saliva** makes humans itch. No wonder people have long fought lice.

Ancient Egyptians, for example, had an imaginative way of avoiding lice. They shaved their heads and wore wigs. That destroyed the **parasites'** homes. A parasite is a creature that lives and depends on another living creature. The creature a parasite lives on is called a host.

Nowadays, we know that lice can sneak rides on combs and hats. So don't share them!

Thirsty Critters

You have probably heard people say, "Don't let the bedbugs bite." You may have wondered if bedbugs are real. They are.

Bedbugs are small, wingless insects. A fully grown bedbug is about the size of an eraser on a pencil. These critters hang out in bedding, clothes, firewood, and luggage.

Like lice, bedbugs drink human blood. Yet that's not the real problem with bedbugs. When a bedbug bites, it puts saliva into the skin. The saliva causes the area around the bite to swell.

Another small parasite can cause even bigger problems. Ticks are related to mites and spiders. They have eight legs. Ticks hitch rides aboard mice, deer, people, and other hosts.

Ticks don't come alone. They carry lots of germs. When a tick bites, those germs may sneak into the host's blood. That can cause problems, including Lyme disease.

Of course, bedbugs and ticks seem almost cuddly next to hookworms and tapeworms.

Hooked on You

Unlike bedbugs or ticks, hookworms don't just bite. These small, round worms chew their way right through the skin.

Once inside the body, this invader makes its way to the intestines. Those are long body parts shaped like tunnels. Stretched out, they would be nearly 30 feet long. The intestines turn food into chemicals that your body needs.

A hookworm bites into the wall of the intestine. It can then hang on for years. That can cause the host big trouble.

Another kind of worm also hangs out in the intestines. It's the tapeworm. The tapeworm is the largest of all our body beasts. It can grow as long as the intestines themselves!

The tapeworm's head has a crown of hooks. They lock onto the intestine wall. The rest of the worm's body floats in the tunnel. As food flows by, the tapeworm soaks it up. That robs the host of **nutrients** and can cause illness.

Mites. *These worm-like critters could fit on the period ending this sentence. They live in skin pockets that hold eyelashes and hairs.*

© DAVID M. PHILIPS/SCIENCE SOURCE

Tick. *This wee hitchhiker slurps blood. During meals, it swells up like a balloon.*

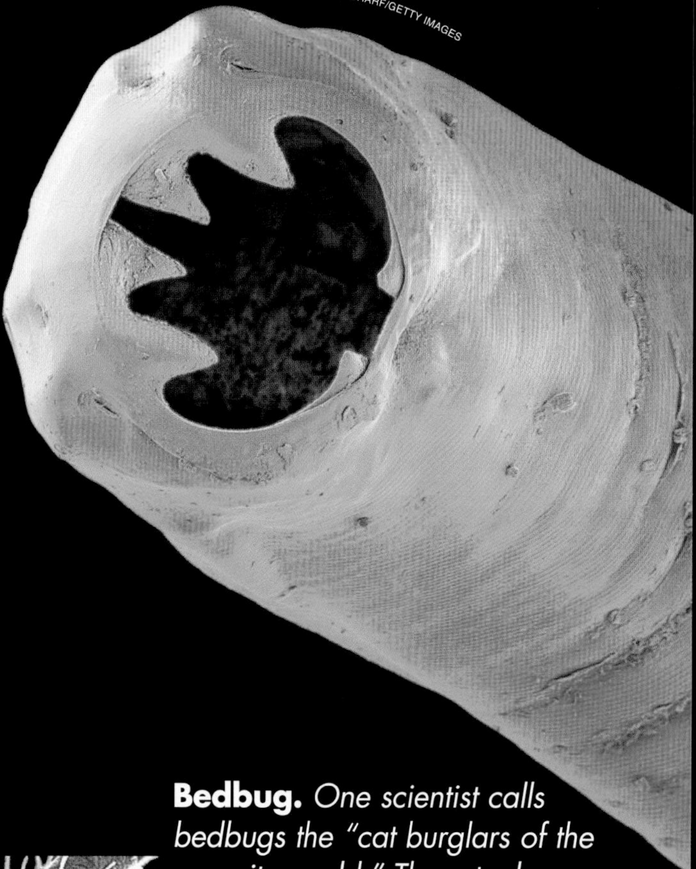

© DAVID SCHARF/GETTY IMAGES

Hookworm. *Lurking in sand or soil, hookworms wait to touch an animal or person. Then they nibble through the host's skin.*

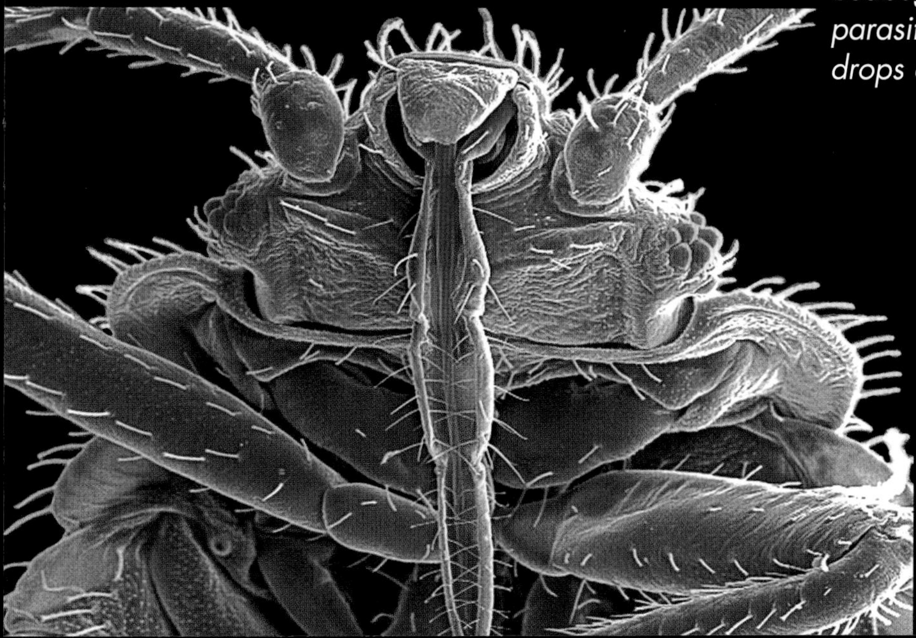

© KALLISTA IMAGES/GETTY IMAGES

Bedbug. *One scientist calls bedbugs the "cat burglars of the parasite world." They steal drops of blood while we sleep.*

Small Crowd

By now, you may be totally grossed out. But fear not. Some body beasts help their hosts.

Take **bacteria,** for instance. Bacteria are tiny living things. They are neither plants nor animals. They are simply bacteria.

Bacteria are some of the smallest living things on Earth. Each has only one **cell.** A cell is the smallest unit of life.

You might think of cells as building blocks. Every living thing is made up of them. Humans have more than ten trillion cells.

Bacteria may be small, but they are nearly everywhere. They outnumber every other kind of living thing.

Scientists estimate that 90 to 100 trillion bacteria live on or in some animals. By and large, those hosts are lucky they do.

Good Neighbors

You may be wondering: Can't bacteria make a host sick? Yes, some kinds can. Many, though, are harmless. Some can even help a host in important ways.

Bacteria on skin often act as tiny trash collectors. They help get rid of oil, sweat, and bits of dry skin. They often make a meal out of those things.

Hosts usually can't see bacteria at work, of course. But a host can smell bacteria. As they eat sweat, bacteria make smelly chemicals. The odor isn't pleasant.

Scientists think bacteria may help in other ways. They may serve as a tiny invisible army. After all, the skin is crowded with bacteria. That could make it harder for germs to enter the body and cause an illness.

Still not ready for an "I Love Bacteria" button? Then think about this. Humans cannot digest bread, fruit, vegetables, or other food from plants. Bacteria can. So bacteria in the intestines digest much of our food for us.

A Mite Complicated

Deciding if a body beast is helpful or harmful can be tough. To see how, let's meet the dust mite. This little critter lives on pillows and sheets. It's a cousin to spiders and scorpions.

Dust mites eat tiny bits of dead skin. That drab diet is handy for human beings. Each day, you see, we shed millions of skin cells. Dust mites take care of them.

The tricky part comes later. After eating, dust mites make a lot of waste. That can trigger asthma attacks and allergies.

Big Happy Family?

You may look at plants and animals differently now. You now know that they aren't alone. Millions of tiny creatures live on and in other living things. Even parasites may carry other parasites.

In some way, no living thing is ever truly alone. Being a habitat is just part of being alive.

Wordwise

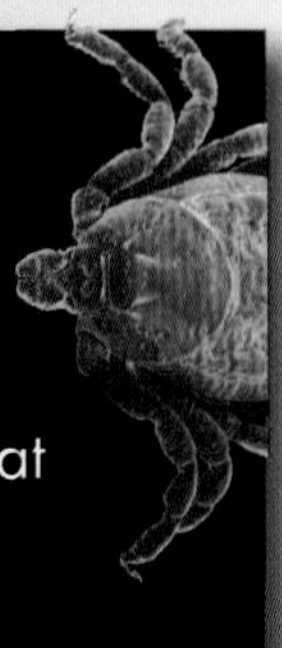

bacteria: tiny living things that are not plants or animals

cell: smallest unit of life

host: plant or animal that is home to a parasite

nutrient: useful chemical in food

parasite: plant or animal that lives and depends on another living thing

saliva: liquid in the mouth

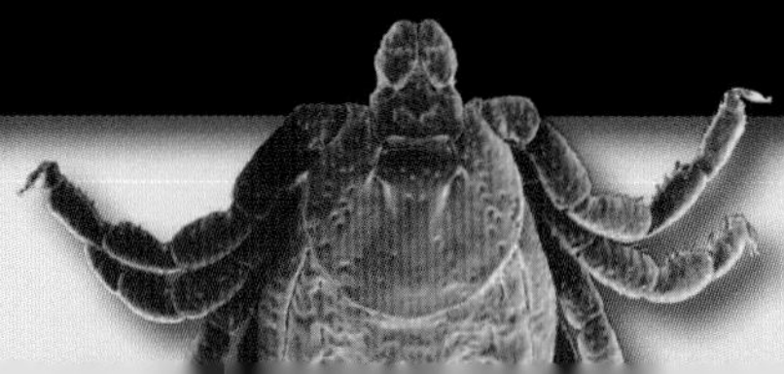

© DAVID M. PHILIPS/SCIENCE SOURCE

Human Habitats

The human body is a world of habitats for tiny living things. This picture shows where some of our invisible neighbors live.

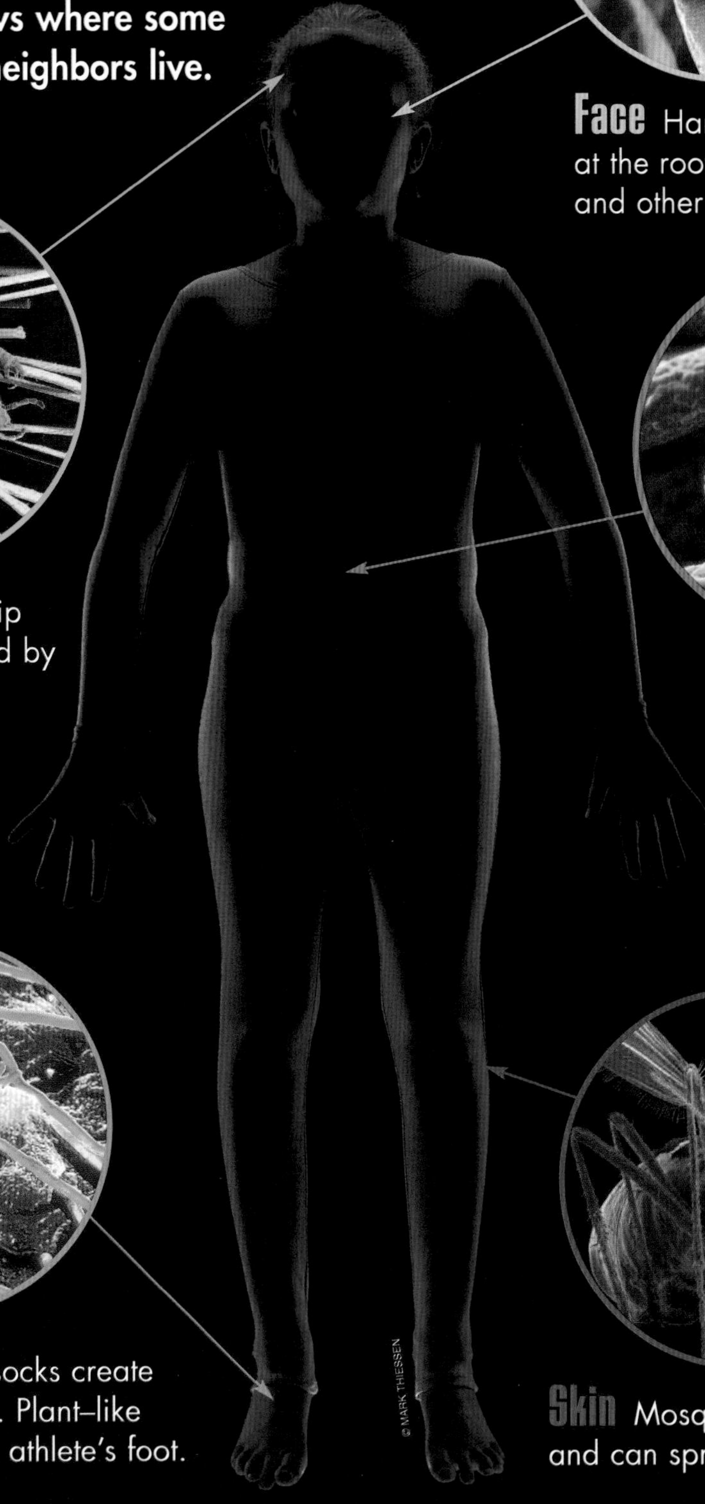

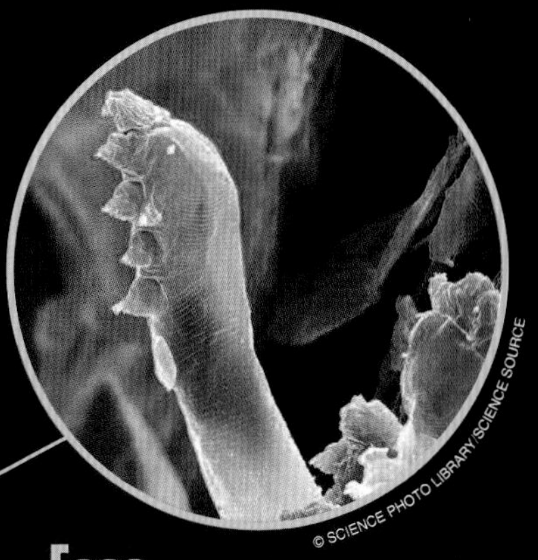

Face Harmless mites live at the roots of eyelashes and other hairs.

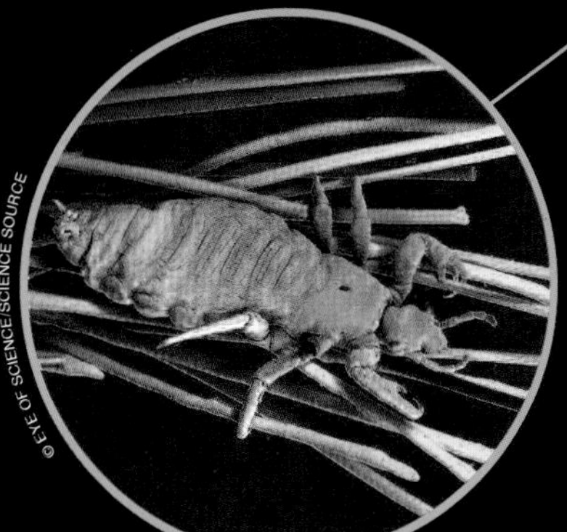

Hair Head lice grip onto hair. They feed by biting the skin and drinking blood.

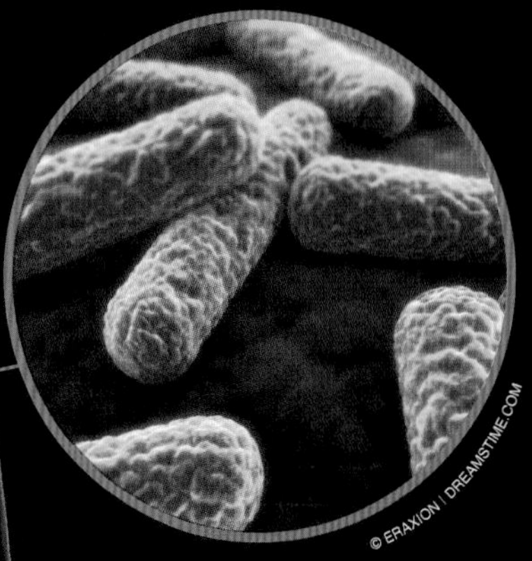

Intestines Bacteria live in these long tunnels. They break down vegetables and grains for us.

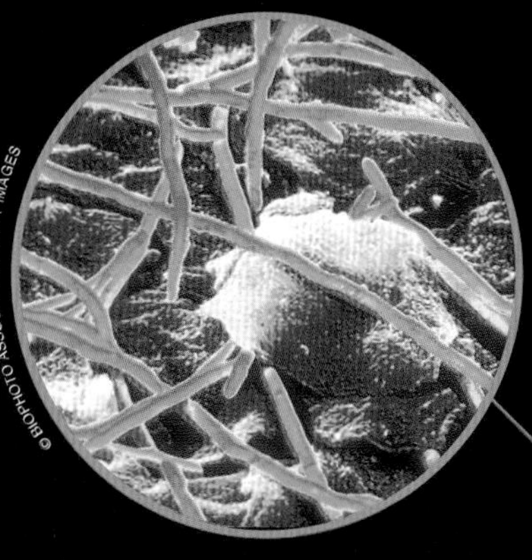

Feet Shoes and socks create warm, moist areas. Plant-like growths can cause athlete's foot.

Skin Mosquitoes take blood and can spread disease.

Seeing

Super Sight. *Scientists use an SEM to discover details of mites. These would be impossible to see with just their eyes alone.*

© SCOTT BAUER/USDA

Tiny Creatures

Most of the creatures that live on your body are tiny. You can't see them just by peering at your skin. So how do we know what they look like? Technology helps us take a closer look.

One tool scientists use is called a scanning electron microscope, or SEM. This is a very powerful tool. It makes things look up to 200,000 times larger than life.

Amazing Pictures

How does an SEM work?

The first step is for scientists to take a tiny creature and coat it with a thin layer of metal. The metal sticks to the bug. Then scientists put the critter into the SEM.

Now the fun begins.

The SEM shoots a beam of tiny particles called electrons at the creature. The beam moves back and forth over the beast. As it moves, electrons from the beam bounce off the bug's new metal covering.

The SEM counts these bouncing electrons. Then it uses this data to make a picture of the creature.

What a picture it is! The SEM shows amazing details that scientists might never have seen before.

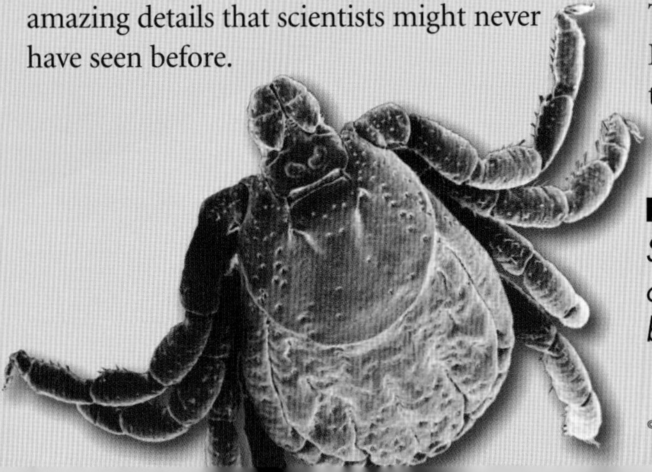

Fabulous Features

What exactly do the pictures show? For one thing, they explain just how body beasts get under your skin. Some bugs have body parts that can saw through your skin. Others have mouths like a doctor's needle. They slip into your skin and suck your blood.

The SEM also shows how bugs find their way to you. Some have enormous eyes to spot you. Others have sensors that tell when a person is near. Some may have wings to help them fly. Others have legs that grab and hold.

Each of these features helps an animal find and feed on a human host.

New Tools, New Insights

SEMs have changed the way people look at body beasts. But the science of seeing doesn't stop there. Scientists still have many questions. How does each bug survive? What does it eat? Where does it have its young?

They also want to know how tiny parasites affect their human hosts. What bugs can make a human sick? How can people get rid of them? The more scientists know about body beasts, the better. With the help of SEMs, scientists are finding answers.

People continue to build better microscopes. They find new ways to see tiny living things. Every new tool helps us learn about the bugs that make humans their home.

Picture Perfect. *This picture from an SEM shows everything from the shape of a tick's legs to the curves of its blood-slurping mouth.*

A Closer Look

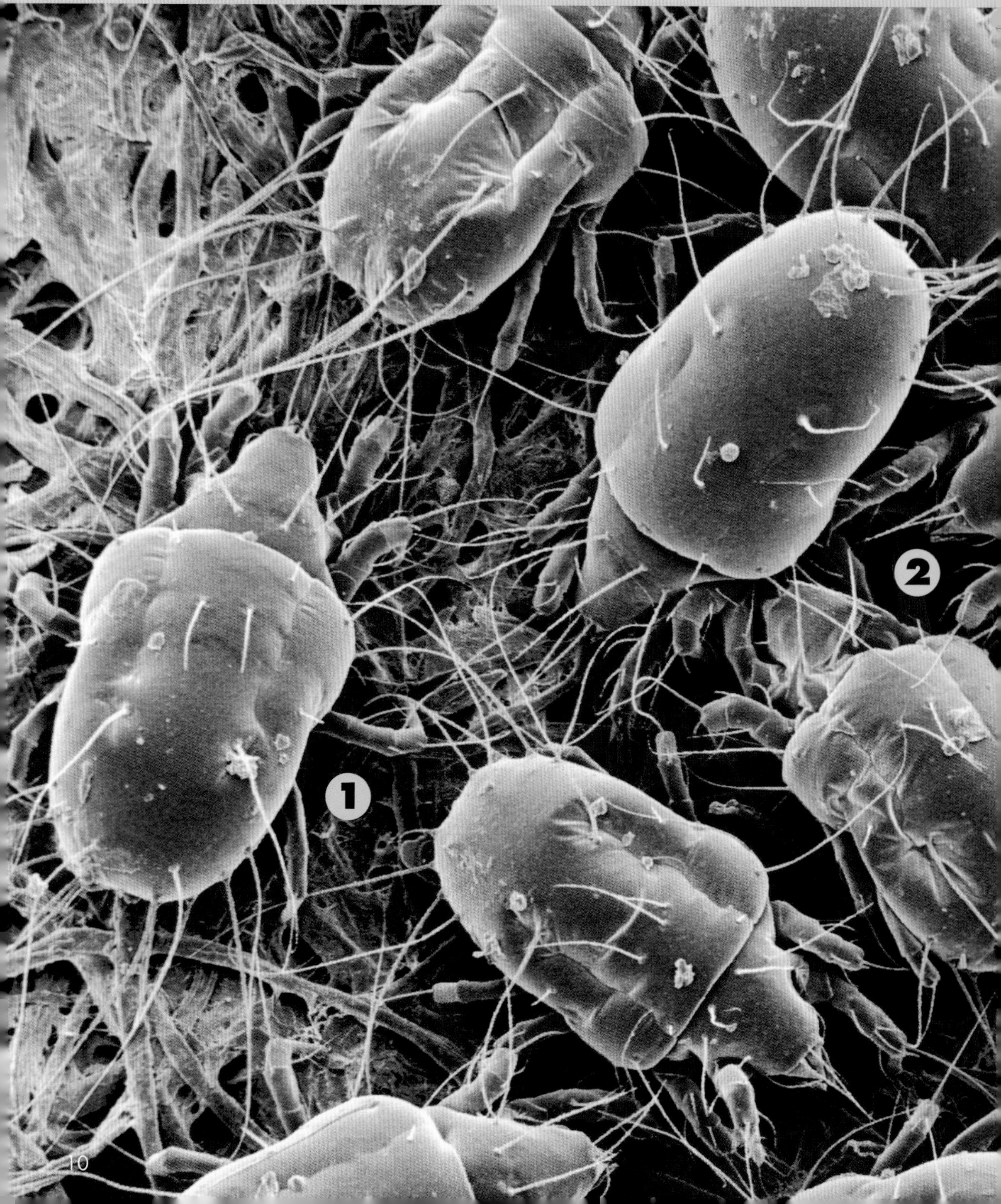

Mites are tiny critters with some amazing features. Take a look at what the scanning electron microscope shows us about these mini-beasts.

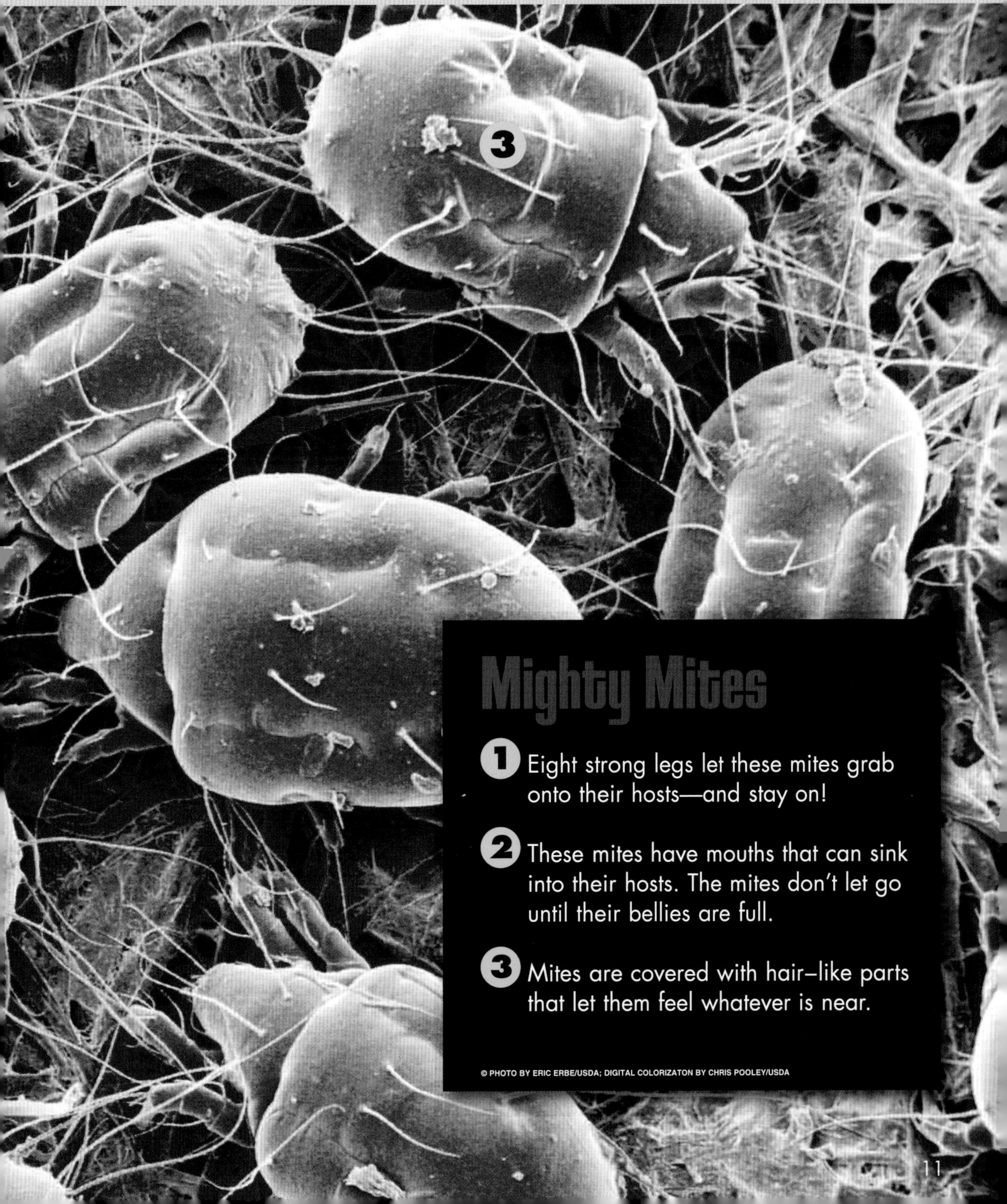

Mighty Mites

1. Eight strong legs let these mites grab onto their hosts—and stay on!

2. These mites have mouths that can sink into their hosts. The mites don't let go until their bellies are full.

3. Mites are covered with hair–like parts that let them feel whatever is near.

Human Parasites

How much do you know about the creatures that call your body home?

1. What is a parasite? What is a host?

2. How do parasites get nutrients from your body?

3. How do bacteria help people?

4. How do SEMs help scientists learn about tiny creatures?

5. Compare two parasites. List the ways they are alike. Explain how they are different.

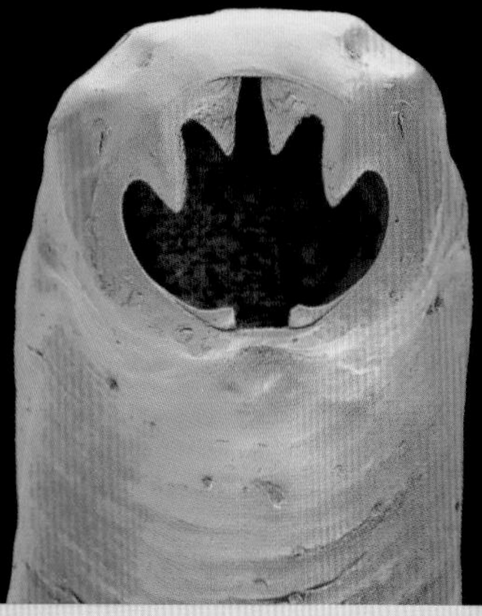